YOUR PLAYBOOK FOR LIVING A

BRAVE LIFE™

WRITTEN BY ALLEGRA COHEN

BRAVE LIFE

Copyright © 2025 by Allegra Cohen
All rights reserved. No part of this publication may be reproduced, stored in a retrieval system, or transmitted in any form or by any means—electronic, mechanical, photocopying, recording, or otherwise—without prior written permission from the publisher, except in the case of brief quotations used in reviews or articles.

Your Playbook For Living A BRAVE LIFE™
Written by Allegra Cohen
First Edition, 2025
Published by Brave Life™ Press
Edited by Rea Frey
Cover and interior design by Anastasia John-Sandy
Production support by Samantha Shaw, Founder of Assist-her.com
Illustrations sourced from royalty-free image libraries

micro-JOYS®, FUNgineer® are registered trademarks of ABUNdance by Allegra Cohen, LLC.
ABUNdance™, and BRAVE LIFE™ are trademarks of ABUNDANCE by Allegra Cohen, LLC.
This book is intended for educational and inspirational purposes only and is not a substitute for professional medical, psychological, or therapeutic advice.

Printed in the United States of America
ISBN: 9798993014708
www.allegracohen.com

For Aston
You are my reason, my reminder, and my reward.
Being brave led me to you—and you are joy itself.

To everyone who has ever reminded me to dance through the hard stuff, laugh in the in-between, and choose joy anyway—thank you.

To my family and dearest friends,
your love has been my anchor and my inspiration.

To every brave soul I've worked with, coached, or cheered on—you are the reason this book exists. Your stories, your hearts, and your light inspire me every day.

To the little girl inside me who kept believing joy was the way—this one's for you.

And to you, sweet reader—thank you for saying yes to joy.

WELCOME TO
BRAVE LIFE™

Welcome, *beautiful soul.*
You're holding the ultimate permission slip to live fully, play often, and feel wildly alive. Braving life isn't about being fearless; it's about dancing with fear and still saying **YES.** Flip through for a spark of joy, read cover to cover, or open to any page when you need a little love, courage, or clarity.

TODAY IS A

GREAT

DAY!

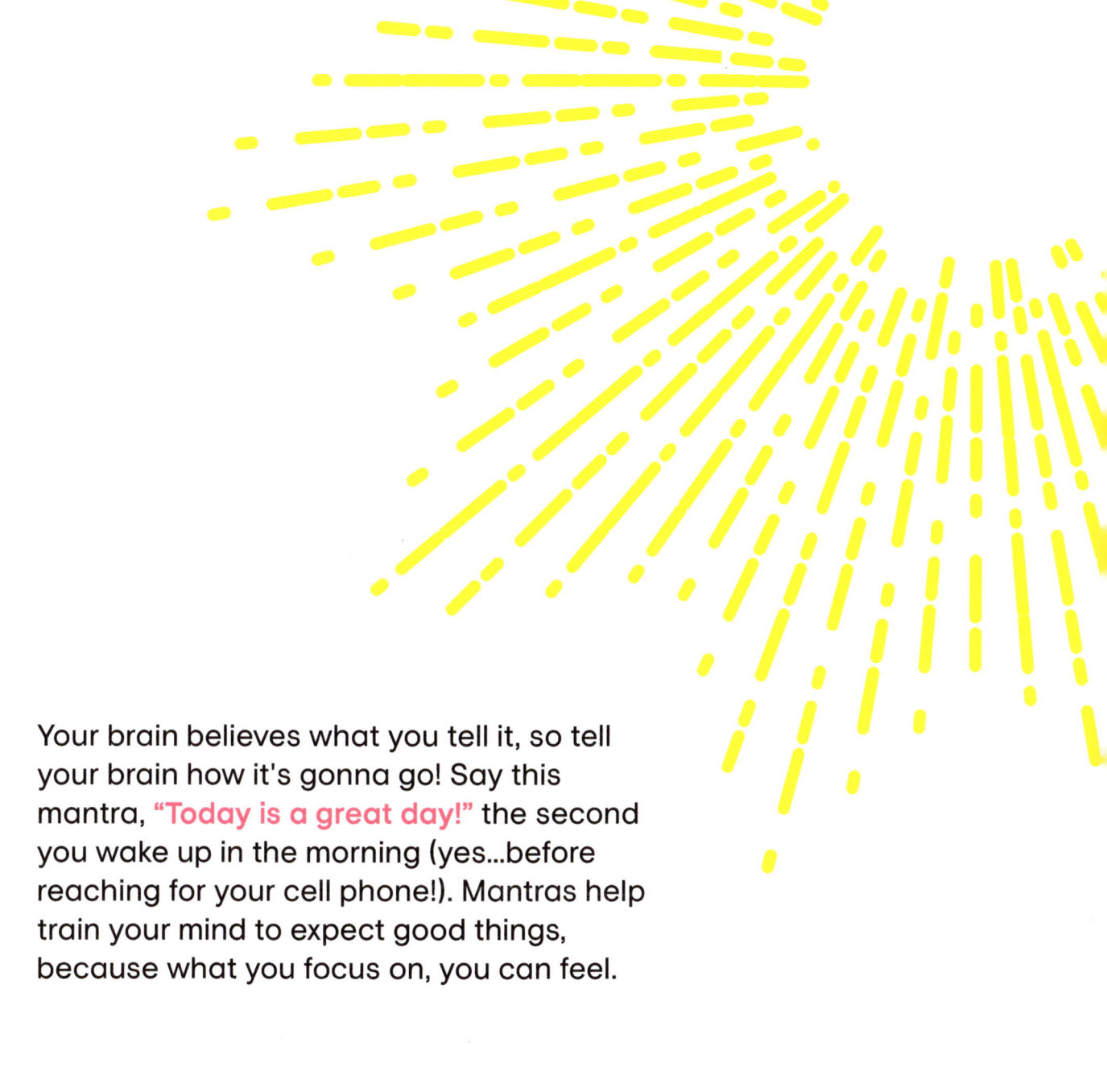

Your brain believes what you tell it, so tell your brain how it's gonna go! Say this mantra, "Today is a great day!" the second you wake up in the morning (yes...before reaching for your cell phone!). Mantras help train your mind to expect good things, because what you focus on, you can feel.

Turn your morning coffee, your skincare routine, or your walk outside into sacred moments of presence. **How?** Slow it down. Feel the warmth of the mug in your hands, breathe in the scent, feel the sun on your face. Let your everyday moments love you back.

THE DAILY
RICHual™

THE abunDANCE

RAISE YOUR FUN FREQUENCY!

When in doubt, dance it out. Your body is your best reset button; shake, smile, breathe, stretch. These moves aren't about choreography, they're about chemistry. Movement shifts your mood, boosts your energy, and tells your brain: **we're choosing joy now.** Do it full out (like you mean it!), and watch your whole vibe rise.

COLLECT
micro-JOYS®

The tiniest joys—a breeze, a giggle, a perfectly ripe avocado—can transform your whole state of being. Notice, savor, and stick them in your back pocket. Collect as many as you can each day! **The secret?** Slow down. Stay curious. Let yourself be surprised by the beauty hiding in plain sight. Joy loves to show up when we are open to seeing it.

PEP TALKS FOR THE WIN

Give yourself a compliment in the mirror. Say, **"You are bold. You are brilliant. You slay."** Because how you speak to yourself becomes how you see yourself. When you uplift your own spirit, you stop waiting for outside validation and you own your magic from the inside out. Talk to yourself like your own hype girl. Watch your fierceness unfold.

Go into each day with the daily intention of giving someone a compliment. Step out of self and into service. Watch how this action creates a micro-JOY for you! **Because when you make someone feel seen, you both light up.**

MAKE SOMEONE'S DAY

Say this out loud:
"I am brave. I am kind. I am proud of myself."
Talk to yourself throughout the day for a quick boost! This isn't just a mirror moment—it's an all-day soul support system. Speak kind words to yourself as you walk, drive, or do the dishes; it pulls you right back into your heart.

A FUNgineer doesn't wait for joy, **she creates it.** She sprinkles play into the everyday, lets curiosity lead, and dance with uncertainty like it's part of the plan. This mindset isn't about ignoring reality, it's about **shifting your energy** so you can face it all with more resilience and spark. You don't have to be perfect, just willing. Wonder is your way in.

REMEMBER THE LITTLE YOU INSIDE

She's still in there. Curious, sensitive, and full of wonder. Listen to her. Protect her. Honor her. Love her like she's the most important person in the world. **Because she is.** Place your hands over your heart. Take a breath. She's always there, grateful for your attention.

Positive energy is magnetic. You are your own wifi signal, so **choose your frequency wisely.** Your energy enters the room before you do; it's in your posture, your tone, and your thoughts. So pause, reset, and realign. Dance it out, shake it off, smile, or take a power nap. Just like wifi, your signal reaches others instantly. You're the hotspot, so set the tone.

Emotions are like weather systems; they roll in, move through, and shift with awareness. You are the weather. **What forecast are you offering?** Pause. Close your eyes. Take a deep breath. Ask yourself: What's my emotional forecast right now? Is it sunny? Stormy? Cloudy with a chance of tears? Whatever it is, meet it with kindness. Then choose one gentle thing that could brighten your sky. A smile. A stretch. A moment of gratitude. Tiny shift, new forecast.

VISUALIZE,
QUEEN

Picture your highest, most radiant self. She walks with purpose, speaks with love, shines without shrinking. What is she wearing? How does she move? Now act like her. Talk like her. Make choices that she would make. Because the truth is, you're not imagining her. You're remembering who you really are.

POWER
POSE

Stand like HER: feet grounded, hands on hips, heart lifted, chin up. **OWN it.** Hold for a minute (yes, really.) Breathe deeply. Feel your body say, "I've got this." This pose isn't just about how you look, it's how you signal strength to your brain. Confidence is a frequency, and you can tune into it, **on demand.**

Fear says, "You can't." Confidence screams, "You got this!" Guess who gets the mic? The Fearleader plays old reruns of doubt, shame, and playing small. The Cheerleader? She's fresh, fierce, and rooting for your brilliance. Start turning up her volume; every time you choose self-love over self-doubt, she gets louder.

FEARLEADER

VS.

CHEERLEADER

YOUR BEST FEELING THOUGHT

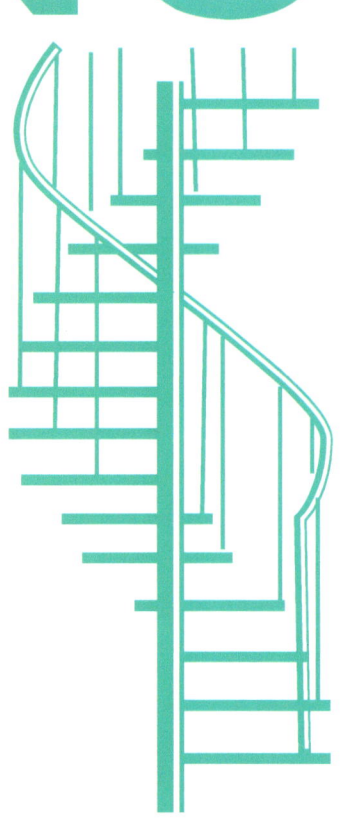

Find the next best-feeling thought. Then the next. That's how you climb the vibe ladder. It's not about pretending everything's perfect; it's about reaching for a thought that feels slightly better than the one before. "I'm stuck" might become "I'm open to new ideas." → "Something always shows up for me." → "I've got this." One gentle shift at a time allows you to rise.

FAITH
IS YOUR SUPERPOWER

You don't have to see the whole path, just the next brave step. Even when the way forward feels uncertain, there is always something holding you, guiding you, even if you can't see it yet. **Faith is quiet courage.** It's trusting there's meaning in the mess and growth in the waiting. Each time you choose faith over fear, something beautiful unfolds within you.

PRESENCE
IS THE
PRESENT

Joy doesn't live in the past or future. It is here now...can you feel it? It's hiding in this very breath. When you slow down and feel your inhale, you return to yourself. When you exhale, you make space for joy to rise. **Your breath is the doorway back to now**—and now is where the magic lives.

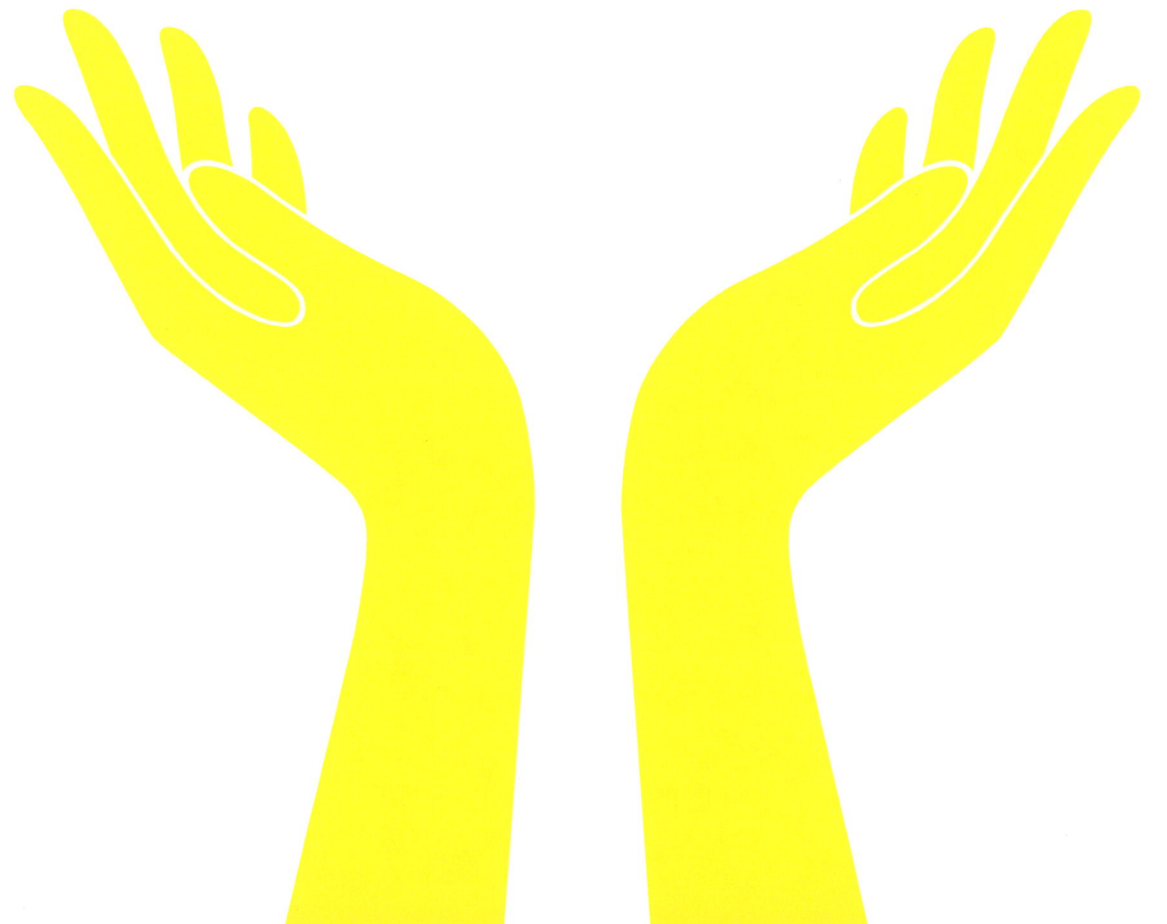

There is always MORE. There's always more love, more time, and more joy. Abundance trusts that the more you give, the more you grow. Start by noticing what's already here. Let gratitude be your gateway.

LOVE IS
BRAVE

Open your heart. Be real. Be seen. Brave love is the kind that lasts. It starts with loving yourself; holding space for your chaos and your crown. The more gently you love yourself, the more fully you can love others. That's the kind of love that heals.

JOY IS
CONTAGIOUS
~SPREAD IT

Your smile is a revolution. Pass it on. And while you're at it, share your micro-JOYS with your people, and ask them to share their micro-JOYS with you. **Their joy becomes your joy!** Joy doesn't need to be loud to make an impact; it just needs to be shared. **Joy is the kind of contagious worth catching.**

THE BRAVE LIFE™
= FULL OUT LIVING

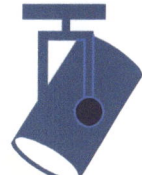

Do life FULL OUT—just like the abunDANCE. No shrinking your joy. **Why?** Because holding back and playing small doesn't protect you—it just dims your light. Living FULL OUT means showing up with your heart open, your energy aligned, and your soul lit. Speak with truth. Live with joy. Love like you mean it.

Every challenge shapes your evolution. **Even the plot twists are gifts.** It's not about pretending the hard stuff isn't hard; it's about trusting that everything has a purpose. When life happens for you, you stop seeing challenges as punishment and start seeing them as invitations to rise. Your growth happens because you moved through the struggle with love, courage, and grace.

BE YOUR OWN
BEST FRIEND

Treat yourself the way you would a best friend. Hype yourself up. Forgive your mess. **Love yourself the loudest.** Why? Because you are the one person who's going to be with you for the rest of your life. Your inner voice becomes your world; make it kind, make it loyal, make it safe. Check in with yourself. Speak to yourself with love. Keep your own secrets. Cheer for your own wins. The relationship you have with yourself sets the tone for everything else.

You are the designer of your experience. **Uplevel your perspective.** This doesn't mean ignoring the hard; it means choosing to see more than the tough stuff. Look for the lesson, the beauty, the growth, or the joy in disguise. When you shift how you see the world, the world begins to shift with you.

LET'S BRAVE LIFE™, TOGETHER

You've got everything you need inside you. You do! **Go shine, play, love, and revel in all of it.** And remember: you were never meant to do it alone. Even the bravest soul needs a hand to hold, a voice of encouragement, and a safe place to land. Reach out. Lean on your support system. Ask for what you need. Your courage gets stronger when it's shared. Braving life isn't a solo mission; it's a soul connection. Let's rise together.

I am here to rise. I was made for this moment.
I am healthy, brave, growing, and becoming.
Joy is my compass. Love is my power.
Today, I choose to live **FULL OUT.**

You've got this. And I've got you.

With so much love,

Allegra

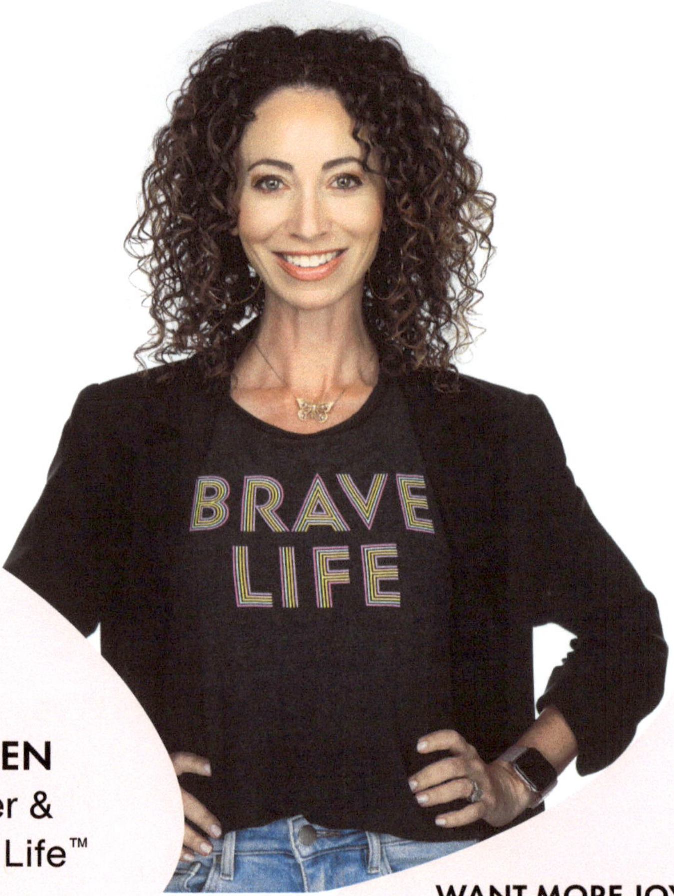

ALLEGRA COHEN
Chief Joy Officer &
Founder of Brave Life™

WANT MORE JOY?
SCAN & EXPLORE BRAVE LIFE™

FOLLOW ALONG & CONNECT:
INSTAGRAM: @ALLEGRACOHEN
WEBSITE: WWW.ALLEGRACOHEN.COM
LINKEDIN: HTTPS://WWW.LINKEDIN.COM/IN/ALLEGRACOHEN/

ABOUT THE AUTHOR

Allegra Cohen is the Chief Joy Officer and Founder of BRAVE LIFE™, where she empowers individuals, from children to professionals, to cultivate self-reliant joy, confidence, and resilience through her signature micro-JOYS® method. She is an award-winning film producer, voiceover artist, and creator of a science-backed approach to transforming everyday moments into real resilience and joy.

As a leading speaker for the U.S. Navy's Warrior Toughness Initiative, Allegra guides the nation's bravest in tapping into imagination, renewal, and connection, proving that bravery isn't just about grit, but about coming home to ourselves. She has been featured on FOX-5 Good Day DC, NBC-10 Boston, and FOX-29 Good Day Philadelphia, and was honored with GlamourGals' Inspiration Award for empowering women nationwide.

A thriver with Crohn's Disease, Allegra brings contagious energy, practical tools, and a whole lot of heart to help people stress less, play more, and lead braver, lighter lives. Her work has impacted thousands across schools, seminars, and organizations, and she recently secured her first TEDx talk.

Above all, Allegra's greatest joy is her family. She's married to her person, David, and is the proud mommy to Aston and bonus mom to Jacob and Eden, her daily reminders that the brave life starts at home.

www.ingramcontent.com/pod-product-compliance
Lightning Source LLC
Chambersburg PA
CBHW051514110526
44582CB00007B/121